PICTURE HISTORY

FOOD

IN HISTORY

Sheila Robertson

First published in 1983 by
Wayland (Publishers) Limited
49 Lansdowne Place, Hove
East Sussex BN3 1HF, England

© Copyright 1983 Wayland (Publishers) Ltd

ISBN 085078 309 7

Series design by Behram Kapadia

Phototypeset by Kalligraphics Limited, Redhill, Surrey
Printed in Italy by G. Canale & C.S.p.A., Turin
Bound in the U.K. by The Pitman Press, Bath

PICTURE HISTORY

FOOD
in History

PICTURE HISTORY

CLOTHES
EXPLORATION
FARMING
FOOD
HOMES
LANDSCAPE
MACHINERY
RECREATION
RELIGION
SCHOOLS
SHOPS
TRANSPORT
WARFARE

Contents

Introduction

To discover what people have chosen to eat through the ages is a very good way of studying man's history. It shows you the effect of climate and geography on his way of life, and it explains a great deal about the rise and spread of civilizations. It can tell you more about the kind of people our ancestors were than the history of wars and politics. It is also a fascinating subject even if you are 'not interested in history' at all.

The effect of food on man's history cannot be exaggerated. It was meat that brought the ape-man down from the trees to forage and hunt on the open plains, thus encouraging him to walk upright, leaving his hands free to use as tools. It was cereals like wheat and maize that persuaded him to cultivate them and give up his wandering life to live in settled communities. It is not accidental that the first civilizations began in those parts of the world where the seasons were marked and corn ripened in a few months. The corn, together with fruits and vines, could be dried and preserved for winter food, and so feed large communities, or be traded for other goods.

Animals were first domesticated in more temperate regions, in a band stretching from Britain across Europe and the Asian steppes to China. Inside this band, the first wild goats, sheep, oxen and pigs were tamed to give milk and meat.

The food we have chosen to eat has given us the power of life and death over the animals and plants. By choosing to eat certain plants or animals we have preserved them from extinction, and by rejecting others, we have condemned them to death. Grains and other seed-bearing plants now depend on man entirely, for they cannot shed their seed without his help. Our domestic animals do not look anything like their forebears. They are bred for meat and milk, and their horns and tusks have disappeared, their legs have become shorter, and their bodies fatter.

This book gives twenty-four examples of the way food has influenced, or been influenced by history. Although I try to give the origin of most of these foods, it is important to understand that it is the origin of their cultivation, rather than where they first grew, that can be traced, and even that is usually most uncertain. Most of the history of any animal or plant had already happened before man appeared on the earth, let alone before he discovered a way of recording his way of life, and the food he ate.

I wish to record my debt to the eminent authority on food, Mr Waverly Root, whose book *Food* is the source of much information contained in the following pages. I would recommend this book, and others by him, to anyone who wishes to study the subject further.

Hunting the Buffalo

Here is an exciting picture of Cheyenne Indians hunting bison from horseback with bows and arrows. It illustrates a major part of the story of evolution.

Millions of years ago one of the ape-like, plant-eating creatures inhabiting the forests acquired a taste for meat. He began by collecting grubs from under stones, robbing birds' nests for fledgelings, and stealing the new-born fawns, lambs, and kids of the placid hoofed animals. He went on to become a hunter of bigger, faster game, and gradually over millions of years his body slowly adapted to its new needs. Because hunting is more successful in groups, they joined families together to form a tribe. The search for better hunting grounds led to the discovery of other territories, and even continents. He began to domesticate animals, first the dog, and later the horse, to help him in the hunt.

Civilization Begins

Meat is highly nutritious. Instead of spending all his waking hours in the search for enough fruit and vegetables to keep him going through the following day, man now had time on his hands. He acquired new skills and crafts, such as cleaning and drying animal skins, sewing warm clothing, and inventing superior hunting weapons, such as the bow and arrow.

Later, people learned to domesticate animals such as cattle, pigs, sheep, and goats to supply their meat needs, but this was not possible everywhere.

Thundering Herds

Although the bison is an ox he cannot be domesticated, partly because his sheer size requires a great deal of food and he needs an enormous territory on which to graze. So he had to be hunted. On the American continent there was plenty of territory and plenty of bison. It is believed that when the New World was discovered by Europeans in the fifteenth century, there were sixty million of them: more than any other species of large animal (except humans) in the world's history. When a herd travelled over the plains one bison could not stop or change direction because there were hundreds of thousands of others in front and behind him.

Three hundred years after the discovery of America there was hardly a bison left. This is not because they were hunted for meat. They were a nuisance to the new settlers in the continent, who needed grazing land for their cattle, and unrestricted passage for roads and railways. Most of all, the new Americans wanted to get rid of the native Indians, who relied on the bison for their food, clothing, shelter and, indeed, survival.

12

A Room of Fruits

This is an illustration to a story about a man called Abu Hasan, in one of the world's most famous books. *The Thousand and One Nights* is a collection of Arabian folk-tales which are at least a thousand years old. Such stories can be just as good a source of finding out how people lived long ago as the most learned history books. You only need to glance at this picture to discover the favourite foods of desert-dwelling Arabs a thousand years ago.

We can clearly see bananas, oranges, melons, grapes, figs and dates. These luscious fruits are much appreciated in hot desert lands or humid countries.

Bananas, which came originally from India, were being cultivated in the Middle East and northern Egypt by the seventh century A.D. The Moslems' holy book, the *Koran*, also written in the seventh century and based upon the Old Testament, lists the banana, not the apple, as the forbidden fruit in the Garden of Eden.

Oranges from China

Oranges were first cultivated in China at least 3,500 years ago. They took two thousand years to reach India, and were not enjoyed by Arabs until several hundred years later. They then spread along the north African coast, and were introduced into Europe via the Moorish invasion of Spain, between the eighth and twelfth centuries.

Melons originated in the Middle East, probably in Persia or Afghanistan, at least 5,000 years ago. The melon was only about the size of an orange in those days, but contained about 94 per cent water and was therefore the perfect fruit for dry, hot countries.

Grapes are another native of Persia, where they have been cultivated since prehistoric times. Not all grapes are suitable for turning into wine, and we may be sure that the ones pictured here certainly were not, for the Moslem religion forbids drinking it.

Fruit of the Desert

Figs have been cultivated in the Middle East for at least five thousand years. They are an especially important crop, which grow in a soil too poor for cereals.

Dates originated in either Africa or Mesopotamia in prehistoric times. In many countries, dates are the main source of food. Each tree produces 300 to 600 lbs (135–270 kilos) of dates, and the yield per acre is about twelve times that of corn.

Unhappily this delicious feast prepared for Abu Hasan caused him a lot of misery. But it would be rather improper to explain why. You must read the story for yourself.

14

The Wheat Harvest

Wheat has been cultivated for at least eight thousand years, and for the first 7,800 of those years it was cut with a sickle or scythe held in the hands. But in England in 1801 a reaping machine was patented, and in 1822 the basic design was invented which all later models copied up to very recent times. A Northumberland schoolmaster, Henry Ogle, was the designer. His machine successfully combined a shearing action (instead of a scything one), with a device to hold the stalks of corn against the cutting blades. This reaper was pulled by horses, and later by tractors. In this photograph, taken in about 1920, two tractors are pulling a binding reaper through the wheat. The revolving reel has six shafts which alternately pull forward a clump of growing wheat and press it against the teeth of the shears. On the near side of the machine you can see the binder, an arrangement for tying the wheat into bundles (called sheaves) and depositing them on the ground.

Origins

Wheat is an important crop and more wheat is eaten than any other food. One fifth of all the world's agricultural land is cultivated for wheat. It is a most adaptable plant, and it is difficult to find conditions in which it cannot grow.

It was growing in Iraq more than eight thousand years ago, and in China at least five thousand years ago. But wheat began so early, and has adapted and spread itself so readily, that its true history is impossible to trace. For one thing it cross-breeds easily with other cereals. In the early days, farmers would hardly notice, or care, if other strains of cereals were growing among their wheat, so that even today when a farmer sows a field he cannot be sure which strain will be harvested.

The Machine Age

Wheat came late to Britain, in about the seventh century A.D., and for another thousand years was eaten less than barley, oats or rye, which were easier to grow in the heavy, damp soil. When agricultural methods began to improve greatly in the eighteenth century, and the yield of wheat increased each year, a lot of attention was given to the task of gathering the harvest more quickly.

Before the reaper was invented, fields were covered for days by dozens of men with scythes. Now two or three men can harvest the crop in a single day. More than anything else, it was the invention of agricultural machinery that took the workers from the land and put them into the factories, forever changing the pastoral and economic life of Britain and the rest of the industrial world.

Flooded Fields

In Europe and America crops grow in well-drained earth. Throughout millions of acres of the Far East, however, they grow in mud and water. For rice flourishes in tropical climates where there are long periods of flooding from monsoon rains.

5000 Years of Rice

In the background of the picture you can see the foothills of a mountain range in China. The rain flows off down the mountain but before it can drain into the Yangtze River it collects in reservoirs and is channelled out to the rice fields. At certain times of the growing season the fields are deliberately flooded, and drained, and flooded again, to imitate the conditions of the monsoon. The working conditions are uncomfortable, but the growers have had time to get used to it: rice has been grown in the Far East for more than five thousand years.

Nobody can be sure where the grass known as rice first appeared in the world, but it was probably in eastern India or Thailand. From its starting point it may have taken several thousand years to spread throughout China, Malaysia, Indonesia, Burma and the Philippines, following the trail of the monsoon rains.

In the Far East, wherever rice became established it became the most impor-tant cereal crop, and often the only food of most people. It is so much part of the culture of these countries that the words 'rice' and 'food' mean more or less the same thing. In Japan the three meals of the day are known as 'morning rice', 'afternoon rice', and 'evening rice'. In Thailand you cannot say 'Come and eat', you have to say, 'Come and eat rice'.

Europeans had never seen rice until Alexander the Great reached India, the eastern extent of his great conquering march in about 326 B.C. It took another thousand years before it was grown in Europe, brought into Spain by the Moors in the eighth or ninth century. After another few hundred years it was being grown in Italy, and then it slowly spread to the rest of Europe.

Rice in the New World

Rice was soon carried to the New World. After attempts were made to grow it in the coastal, swampy regions of South Carolina, it began to flourish. Two hundred negro slaves were imported to America from Barbados in 1671 to work in the rice fields. By 1820 South Carolina produced half of all the rice grown in the United States.

Today, America is the world's biggest exporter, sending back several billion tonnes of rice a year to the countries where it all began.

The Oldest Food

It is difficult to tell which food is the world's third oldest, but there is no doubt about the first and second. Milk is essential to humans and mammals in the first days of life, but it is undoubtedly beaten into first place by a substance which is necessary to *all* animal life. Animal life began in the sea and, even today, the proportion of salt in our blood is about the same as in sea water.

Salt is collected in many ways and from various sources, but its origin is always the sea. This picture shows a European ship's company somewhere in the tropics (note the palm trees), who have temporarily anchored in order to collect some salt. From earliest times man has understood how essential salt is to the diet. It is also valuable for preserving meat and other food, and the salt the sailors are gathering is almost certainly for that purpose.

A Salty Harvest

From the top left-hand corner the sun is shining down upon the sea, slowly evaporating the water but leaving behind the salt. However, the ship's company cannot wait quite so long, so they have constructed a series of shallow troughs, and run sea water into them to hasten the process of evaporation. As the brine becomes thicker the sluice gate is opened and it is run off into another trough, and then into further ones, until it has dried sufficiently to form crystals.

The man at the far side of the trough is scooping out the coarse crystals and piling them in a heap to drain. Down at the bottom, men are making barrels in which the dry salt will be stored.

Underground Mines

Salt was also collected from underground where, many millions of years ago, there were salt seas which have now dried up leaving the salt behind. In Austria there is a salt mine still in use which was being used in the Stone Age and there are a dozen others in Europe dating back to the Bronze Age. All through history, wars have been fought to protect the salt trade from one country to another, and a tax upon salt was one of the commonest ways to raise money.

When the British ruled India they did not let the people gather their own salt, but insisted they buy salt exported from Britain. It led to one of the best-known incidents in India's fight for independence. The revolutionary leader, Gandhi, led a crowd of followers on a symbolic march to the sea to gather salt in a famous gesture of defiance. The universal importance of salt united the Indian peoples more than anything else could have done.

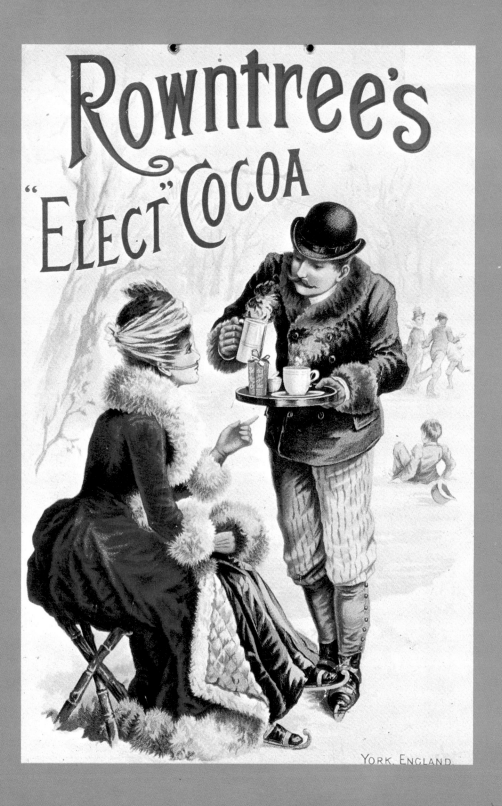

A Cup of Chocolate

The Aztecs used the seeds of the cacao tree as money – until they decided they preferred to eat them. It is difficult to guess how they made this discovery, because turning cacao seeds into a drink (cocoa) or a sweetmeat (chocolate) is an extremely complicated business. Nor can we guess why they even wanted to do it, because chocolate has such an incredibly bitter taste that it is quite inedible without a lot of sugar. Even bitter chocolate contains 30–40 per cent sugar.

However, they managed it, and when the Spanish conqueror Cortez arrived in Mexico in the early sixteenth century, he enjoyed chocolate so much that he took some cacao beans back to Spain. Spain hindered all attempts by other countries to discover the secret of chocolate-making, but then Portugal discovered some cacao trees in its colony Brazil, so they were able to share the monopoly.

From Spain to France

From Spain and Portugal, chocolate moved into France by two quite separate routes. Refugees from Spain settled in southern France and began making chocolate in the town of Bayonne. It was considered a low-class product by the city authorities and they banned its manufacture (or perhaps the reason was that it rivalled other sweetmeats manufactured by local businessmen). The refugees had to move their sordid trade outside the city precincts. But in 1615 Louis XIII of France married the daughter of Philip III of Spain. She introduced chocolate to the French Court, and it quickly became very fashionable.

A Cup of Luxury

The first chocolate house opened in London in 1657, and others followed, setting a fashion for elegant chocolate houses which rivalled the coffee houses which were also springing up. Chocolate was only for the rich, though, because the Government imposed huge duties on it. The duties were not abandoned in Britain until the mid-nineteenth century, just in time for Joseph Rowntree to start up in business.

With his brother, Rowntree began manufacturing cocoa at York in 1869 and continued doing so until he retired in 1923. By then Rowntree's was one of the largest chocolate and cocoa-making establishments in the world. This advertisement captures delightfully the appeal of chocolate, which has always had an atmosphere of festivity and luxury about it. In this advertisement, the gentleman offers the lady a warm, inviting taste of hot cocoa and an enticingly wrapped box of chocolates. His extraordinary generosity is emphasized by the fact that there is only one cup!

The Humble Egg

Every animal begins life as an egg, but the only ones that can be eaten are those from which live young are produced. There are fishes' eggs, many of which are greatly prized by gourmets, such as caviare (the eggs of the sturgeon), the eggs of mullet, and herring. There are the eggs of reptiles, mainly the turtle, but also crocodile eggs which people in the East Indies enjoy.

However, most of the eggs we eat come from birds. As birds are abundant wherever there are trees, fresh water, or sea water, and their eggs are so conveniently packaged, easily collected, extremely nutritious, and either eaten raw or easily cooked it is not surprising that eggs have always been one of man's most appreciated foods. By far the most important bird's egg is the hen's, a specimen of which the lady in the picture is inspecting so closely.

A New Arrival

Although eggs of one kind or another have been eaten since time immemorial, the hen's egg is a fairly recent arrival. Hens are not mentioned anywhere in the Bible, and are not believed to have existed in ancient Egypt either. It was probably in India or China that the jungle fowl was first domesticated in about 2000 B.C.

Homer, who lived in Greece in the tenth century B.C., does not mention them in his epic poems, the *Iliad* and *Odyssey*, but four hundred years later, the people of the ancient Greek city of Sybaris in southern Italy, who were famous for their self-indulgence, passed a law that cocks were not to be allowed in the city because their crowing woke people up too early! So clearly hens had arrived in the Greek world by then, and soon spread to Rome, where the people were already eating peacocks' eggs, or at least the richest were.

A Family Meal

While the Egyptians were waiting for the hen to arrive, they had many other birds' eggs to choose from, including ducks', pelicans' and even ostriches'. An ostrich's egg, weighing about three pounds, was a meal for a large family, and we can assume that they were hunted eagerly over large parts of Africa. Maoris who discovered a moa's egg were even luckier: before that bird became extinct during the seventeenth century, it was laying eggs three times larger than an ostrich's.

Duck and goose eggs are also widely eaten, and other favourites, which vary from country to country, come from penguins, pigeons, gulls, partridges, and plovers. Plovers' eggs were also greatly enjoyed by the American Indians.

23

The Mysterious Pea

Here is a picture of a kitchen garden where a young Victorian woman, helped by her daughter, is picking some peas. She may be a servant preparing a meal for a large number of people, for that nearly-full basket is a rather big one. Or perhaps she intends to dry the peas. Peas keep so well that they used to be stored in case of famine. When this young woman was alive it was believed the pea was a native of southern Europe. Although we now know this is wrong, the pea is still a bit of a mystery.

Unknown Origin

There is plenty of evidence that the pea was a favourite food many thousands of years ago. The oldest discovery of peas was made at an archaeological site on the border of Burma and Thailand, where special carbon date-testing indicated they were more than 11,500 years old. They have also been found in Iraq, at a site three or four thousand years younger. But whether they grew there, or were imported is something we do not know. As peas like a mild climate they probably came from north of these places. We do know they were grown in Greece during the Trojan Wars, and they were being made into soup in the fifth century B.C. But how they crossed the dry deserts of the Middle East is a mystery. They might have been carried by traders, but would have been dried and preserved, which would have made them heavy. One cannot imagine they were valuable enough to pay for the trouble and cost of carrying them so far.

There is evidence of peas in Hungary, Switzerland, France, and England before the birth of Christ. Could this be an indication that they originated in a temperate or high-altitude climate, perhaps in China or northern India, and travelled slowly west until they reached Britain? Their appearance in Iraq and Greece would then have been offshoots from that westerly course.

Fit for a King

It was probably not until the thirteenth century that peas were a common food in Europe. There was some disagreement about whether they were most fit for rich or for poor. There are fashions in food almost as much as in clothes, yet the same vegetable which was considered suitable for the peasants in Germany, was a 'royal dish' presented to Henry II of France by his Italian wife from Florence. One hundred and sixty years later, Madame de Sevigne, the seventeenth-century aristocrat, wrote to her daughter on the subject of peas, '. . . Impatience to eat them, the pleasure of having eaten them, and the longing to eat them again . . .'

A Gift of the Gods

In medieval times and earlier, honey was much more important than it is today, because it was the only sweetener commonly available – sugar was too expensive until later. Honey is the substance manufactured by bees to feed their young: it is more or less pre-digested sugar. The raw material is the nectar from tree blossom or flowers, and the taste of the honey depends on which plant the bee visits. The Greeks of Hymettus, and the Sicilians of Hybla, thought honey a gift of the gods because in those areas the bees fed on thyme. Dwellers in Trabzon on the southern shore of the Black Sea thought honey poisonous, because the bees there fed on a type of azalea (a poisonous plant), and there is a story that the soldiers of Alexander, who were passing that way, suffered a painful illness after eating it.

Stone-Age Food

Honey has been eaten as far back as we can trace. There are Stone-Age paintings on rocks showing men gathering honey from the nests of wild bees. It was during the Bronze Age that men learned how to domesticate bees and encourage them to build their honeycombs where they were easily extracted. Ancient Egyptian bas-reliefs of 4,500 years ago illustrate bee hives. 'A land flowing with milk and honey', is the Biblical expression for a country where life is a pleasure rather than a struggle.

In this picture we see a medieval bee garden, where hives are laid out along the wall with men and women encouraging the bees to nest in them. Outside the walls they are gathering the nests of wild bees from the trees, in order to bring the bees into their own hives.

Honey and Wax

The hives are quite different to the ones you see today, for the people were trying to copy the bees' natural nests. They are made of straw sewed tightly together with cane or bramble. Nowadays they are constructed of frames hung inside a square wooden box. Every manor would have its own bee garden, and so would many poor peasants. The monasteries were the biggest keepers of bee-hives, though for them the beeswax was probably more important than the honey (wax was used to make candles).

There are many varieties of bees, but not all of them produce honey. Others produce rather poor honey, among which were the native American bees. Incas and Aztecs domesticated them, but the first European settlers, the Pilgrim Fathers, imported their own. These soon escaped, and began to spread over the continent.

Food for the Poor

To begin with, the potato was thought fit only for livestock and the very poorest people, even though some of the poor thought it was poisonous and refused to eat it. It eventually became such an important food that the failure of the crop in the nineteenth century caused widespread famine in Ireland. The picture here is probably an illustration for a story in a magazine or book, showing the despair of a poor Irish crofter whose potatoes have been struck by 'the blight'. For years it has been his main food – perhaps his only food – and now he faces starvation.

Drake's Discovery?

Like so many other of our foods, the potato comes from the American continent. In 2000–3000 B.C., Peruvian Indians were growing potatoes in those parts of the Andes too high for maize. The potato travelled slowly, however, not even reaching Mexico before European adventurers began arriving in the New World of America. This somewhat disproves the theory that Drake (or Raleigh) brought potatoes to England from Virginia. If either of them did bring anything back, it was probably the sweet potato, a quite different vegetable. Alternatively they may well have collected potatoes from South America, but the popular belief is that they came from Virginia, because that is where the first English settlement was made.

The Spanish began to grow potatoes in about 1550, and they were grown in Italy soon after. By the end of the seventeenth century, potatoes were grown in every country in Europe, but from dire necessity rather than choice. They were cheap and easy to grow, and therefore considered a good enough food for the poor, although many of the poor thought that potatoes were poisonous, or caused leprosy. In Prussia, Frederick the Great could not persuade his starving subjects to eat them. Nevertheless, wherever there were very poor people with nothing else to eat, potatoes were cultivated.

Irish Famine

Because of Ireland's poverty, potatoes became the most important food there. In 1842 the potato blight struck Germany and spread through Europe, reaching Ireland in 1845. One of the great results of the potato famine was the emigration of two million Irish people over the next twenty years to the United States, although that is not how the potato reached America. It had already been carried there by Irish settlers to New Hampshire in 1719, where it became known as the 'murphy', which was a common Irish name.

29

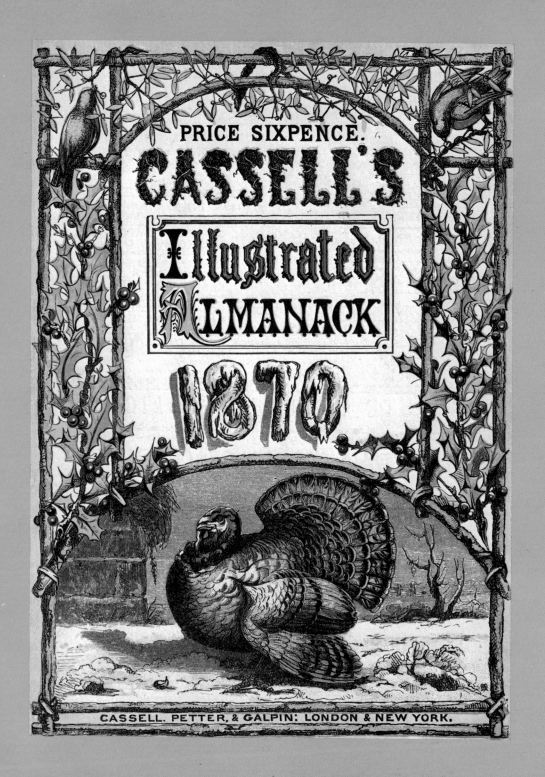

PRICE SIXPENCE.

CASSELL'S

Illustrated Almanack

1870

CASSELL, PETTER, & GALPIN: LONDON & NEW YORK.

A Celebrated Bird

Turkeys do not come from Turkey, and although they used to be known as Indian hens, neither do they come from India. They come from the New World and so were unknown to Europeans and others until, at the end of the sixteenth century the New World was discovered, and gave us potatoes, tomatoes, maize, haricot beans, and our Christmas turkey. You see it here with its traditional companions of robins, holly and snow, drawn on the cover of a nineteenth-century journal.

The credit for bringing the first turkey to Europe is sometimes given to an unknown lieutenant of the explorer Sebastian Cabot in the fifteenth century. It is just possible, because Cabot sailed as far south as Florida in 1499, where turkeys were plentiful. It could also have been the Spanish conqueror Cortez in 1528 although that does not seem likely. At any rate, by about 1530, European kings and merchants were eating turkey and had already forgotten their former passion for peacock.

A Festive Dish

What did people eat at Christmas and Thanksgiving before turkey? For that matter, why is turkey eaten at all on those two festivals?

In the case of Christmas the answer is a mystery. But we know it began early,

because in 1557 Thomas Tusser published his *Hundreth Good Points of Husbandrie* and stated that the turkey was part of the farmer's Christmas dinner. In the case of Thanksgiving, however, the answer is easy. It formed part of the first Thanksgiving Dinner in 1621. After gathering in their first meagre harvest, the European settlers in America celebrated the first year of God's gift of the harvest with a meal, of which an important part was turkey. It has been a traditional part of all Thanksgiving dinners since. Thanksgiving falls on the last Thursday of November.

Protecting the Corn

As with so many other good foods, turkeys originated in Central America. From Mexico, the turkeys penetrated north in such numbers that the Indians of the eastern seaboard states, and the central plains never bothered to domesticate it for food: it was just as easy to go out into the woods to shoot one. It was only in the south-west that turkeys were domesticated, because the Indians there were not nomads but settled communities, tilling their fields of maize. The dry climate there provided little food for wild turkeys (except, of course, the Indians' corn). Turkeys were domesticated in order to protect the fields of crops, rather than as a supply of meat.

Harvest from the Sea

Here is a wood-engraving of a seventeenth-century scene at a fishing port in Newfoundland, in America. Though crudely drawn, it manages to show nearly every aspect of the early fish-processing industry. On the left stands a fisherman dressed in the typical, heavy cloth coat, and leather apron to keep out the cold and wet, holding the hook and baited line on which the cod was caught. This was before the days of trawling with a net, and in the background you can see the men throwing out their lines from the side of their sailing ship. This might seem slow work, but it was possible for one man to catch three or four hundred fish in a day.

Drying and Salting

In the shed on the quay, men are gutting the fish and throwing them into barrels from where they are taken to be salted in the long troughs on the right-hand side of the picture. Two men are carrying a load of fish to be cleaned in an enclosure at the water's edge. Then they are taken to the press, the box-like machine on the right, to have the oil extracted from their livers. Cod-liver oil was used widely in medicines and indeed still is today. You can see a channel leading from the box, carrying the oil into a barrel. Finally the fish are laid out on long tables to dry. Dried and salted cod will keep for years.

There are few places in the world where fish do not form some part of man's diet, and have done so since prehistoric times. Fish is the most plentiful form of food in the world which does not need human aid to flourish. Of all fish, cod is probably the most important. It is certainly one of the world's most prolific breeds, and Alexandre Dumas, the nineteenth-century French writer, once claimed that if every cod's egg conceived was able to reach maturity, it would only be three years before you could walk across the Atlantic on the backs of cod without getting your feet wet!

Norse Fishermen

The cod has been around for a long time. Its remains turn up in archaeological sites dating back to 3000 B.C. It was probably the first fish to be caught commercially, that is to say fished as a form of trade, and Norsemen were likely to have been the first commercial fishermen. As early as the ninth century A.D., Iceland and Norway were selling dried cod to foreign countries, and it was the staple diet of the Vikings on their raiding voyages. The French and Dutch had a flourishing cod industry in the Middle Ages, when fish were eaten much more than they are today, mainly because they were all Catholic countries, and meat could not be eaten on fast days.

Adventure at Sea

At first glance this is a picture of a rescue at sea. Eighteen poor men, who have been drifting in a longboat, are being picked up by a ship with the appropriate name of *Bounty*. They look a jolly bunch of sailors on the *Bounty*; they are even growing little trees in tubs on the deck.

An Important Mission

The truth, regrettably, is less pleasant. Perhaps the ship's name has already given the game away, for the story of the mutiny on the *Bounty* is well known. In December 1787 Captain William Bligh was sent by the British Government on an important mission to the South Seas. He was to collect specimens of the breadfruit tree which flourished there, and transport them to the West Indies where they would be cultivated as a source of cheap food for the slaves.

Bligh was an experienced seaman who had served under Captain Cook, and he was determined to make a success of his voyage. He arrived at the island of Tahiti after ten months at sea, and spent six months collecting the best specimens for transplanting, and then set off for the West Indies. However, those six months on Tahiti with the friendly natives, pleasant weather, and little work to do, had completely demoralized the crew. Bligh was a strict disciplinarian, and the prospect of many long months at sea under his command was too much for the sailors. The last straw came when Bligh cut the men's water ration in order to feed his precious breadfruit trees. The crew mutinied and set Bligh and his officers adrift as you see in the picture, with a few provisions but no navigation chart. They chucked the hated breadfruit trees overboard, and set off back to an island later named Pitcairn. Their descendants still live there.

Success At Last

By an amazingly skilful and courageous piece of navigation, Bligh managed to reach the island of Java, near Timor. This was a journey of 3,618 miles, which they made in forty-eight days. From there he returned to England.

He was sent out again to collect breadfruit, and this time with success. In 1793 his loaded ship arrived in Jamaica, and soon the breadfruit was growing widely. After all that, it was never quite so successful as the authorities had hoped, for the slaves preferred the plantain which already grew there.

Back in the Indian Archipelago and the Pacific Ocean, however, it continues to be the principal diet for many people. It is usually eaten as a vegetable, roasted or baked. Its taste and consistency is a bit like bread: hence its name.

35

Business over Coffee

Soon after coffee was introduced to Britain in the middle of the seventeenth century, coffee houses like this one began springing up all over London and the larger cities. Over the fire hangs a large cauldron of boiling water, and on the hob in front stand four of the black, long-spouted, iron coffee-pots with the coffee infusing and keeping warm until it is called for.

A Cosy Scene

You might imagine that coffee could not be enjoyed without tobacco, for nearly every man in the picture is smoking the long-stemmed, meerschaum pipes, and the few who are not seem about to be served by the boy at the counter. The pleasant scene is cosily lit by the cheerful light of the fire and the many candles on the benches. Even the boy by the fire is enjoying a quick swig of coffee, possibly while the proprietress is not looking!

The first coffee house was opened in Oxford in 1650, and the first in London in 1652. Within forty years there were more than five hundred of them. In the days before telegraph or newspapers, they became regular meeting places for men to exchange the news of the day, and conduct business in a pleasant atmosphere away from their offices. Each coffee house had its own character, and men would have their favourite place to go. Button's and Wills's coffee houses became the centres of the Whig and Tory groups. Many others were the everyday stage for the actors, wits, and literary men of the day.

Lloyd's of London

We do not know which coffee house is pictured here, but it would be nice to think it were Lloyd's. When Edward Lloyd moved his coffee house from Tower Street to Lombard Street in 1692, it grew popular with people in the shipping business. Many of them were in the business of insuring goods brought to England from far-off countries. After a while it became understood that if you had a cargo to insure, or a ship to hire, you went to Lloyd's to do business. The work was conducted, and the contract signed, right there on the benches amongst the litter of pipes and coffee cups. From these humble beginnings, Lloyd's grew to be the world's centre for marine insurance and information.

The coffee tree from which coffee beans come was growing in Arabia in very early times but it did not reach Europe until near the middle of the seventeenth century. Some years later a Dutchman brought the coffee tree to Java and cultivated it in the Dutch colony there. It has since been introduced to many tropical countries.

Herbs and Spices

Here is a picture of a medieval herb garden. Each little square is growing a different herb, of which there are more than twenty to be seen in the picture, and probably many more just outside it. The apothecary (chemist) from the shop across the road is pointing to the herbs, telling the herbalist's head gardener which herbs he will buy. The open window by the house, with the woman sitting by the railing, looks very like a check-out – there might almost be a cash register in the window! Two other servants are carrying the baskets of herbs through the door in the wall and over to the apothecary's shop. Most will bear little resemblance to those your mother uses in the kitchen.

A 'Cure-All'

The word 'herb' in those days meant a plant used to prevent or cure bodily ills. One of the most famous herbals (books describing the properties of herbs), was written by Nicholas Culpeper in the seventeenth century, and listed 369 of them, few of which you would find in your local supermarket. The entry for water-agrimony reads: 'It helps the cachexia, or evil disposition of the body; also the dropsy and yellow jaundice. It opens the obstructions of the liver; mollifies the hardness of the spleen; breaks imposthumes, is an excellent remedy for the third-day ague, provokes urine and the terms, kills worms and cleanseth the body of sharp humours which are the cause of itch , scab, etc.'

The difference between herbs and spices has become blurred, but basically herbs are used fresh, and spices, which come mainly from tropical countries, are used in a dried form. From the dawn of civilization, spices such as pepper, cloves, cinnamon, nutmeg and ginger have been highly valued, cultivated and fought over.

The Spice Trade

For almost fifteen hundred years the Arabs held a monopoly of the spice trade between East and West. The great sea-voyages of Bartholomew Diaz, Vasco da Gama and Christopher Columbus in the fifteenth century were not just undertaken in a spirit of adventure and discovery, but were made to break this monopoly, and to find a quick and cheap route to India where the spices were. Once the sea-route was discovered, and spices were carried in ships instead of overland, political power changed suddenly and dramatically from Arabia to the seafaring nations of Europe. The great empires of the British, French, Spanish and Dutch owed their existence largely to their desire to protect their interests in the spice territories.

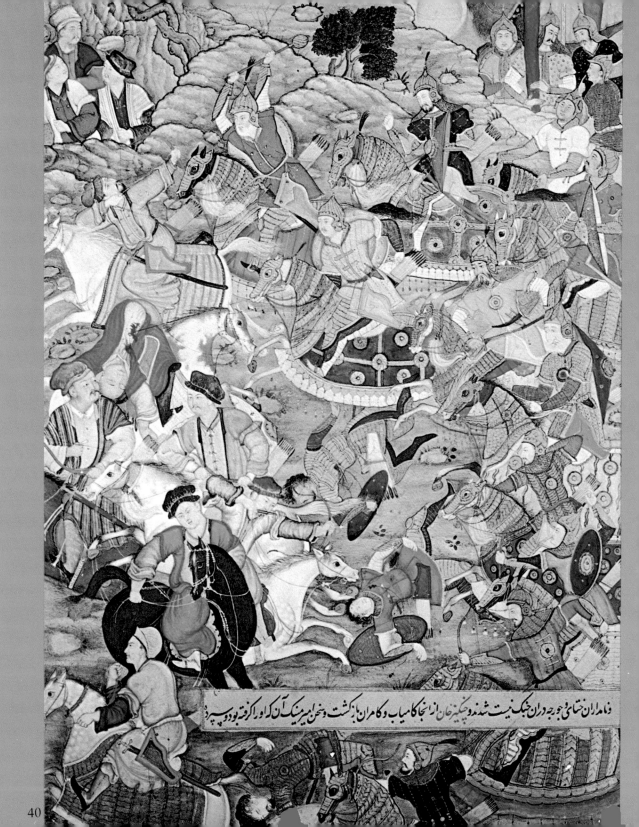

وماهداران ختائی خوربرجه درزان جنگ نبت شدند و جنگیز خان ازانجا کامیاب و کامران بازگشت و سخن امیر سنگ آن که او را فرقته بود و سپرد

40

Milk the Conqueror!

Milk could be called the first food of the world – for it is the first food to pass the lips of every human being. It is the only food essential to life. No baby can live more than a few days without milk, nor can any other mammal. The very word 'mammal' comes from the mammary glands, where milk is produced in the female.

The Sacred Cow

Very early, too, man learned the trick of milking other animals. He was still in the Stone Age between five and ten thousand years ago, when nomads began to roam the Asian steppes with their herds. About 1800 B.C. these Aryan nomads entered India with herds of cows which became so important to the diet and the culture of Indians that the cow became, and remains, sacred.

Milk has affected the rise and the spread of civilizations more than any other food, even wheat, maize or rice. Both Greeks and Romans milked goats and sheep, but used the milk for cheese-making, not to drink. Reindeer, camels, yaks, buffalo and pigs have all been milked too, and all but the pigs are still. And so are horses – which brings us to the picture opposite.

What it illustrates is a battle between the hordes of Genghis Khan, and other Mongolian tribes during Genghis Khan's first great march of conquest upon China in the early thirteenth century. Genghis Khan is probably the greatest conqueror the world has ever seen. After overthrowing the Chinese empire he turned west, and in his lifetime and that of his sons and grandsons, his Mongol hordes held sway across the entire length of Asia and eastern Europe. Undoubtedly two reasons for his success were his brilliance and his ruthlessness, but another reason was milk!

A Supply of Milk

Look again at the horses in the picture. Most of them are mares. The Mongols always rode with a packhorse that would carry leather bags full of their own milk, condensed into a paste-like form, which could keep for weeks or months. So they were ensured a regular supply of food, and with what they could ravage from the country they passed through, they had no need for supply lines. There was nothing to stop their headlong dash across Asia to the gates of Vienna.

In medieval times cows' milk was drunk by rich and poor alike, but never in great quantities because most breeds of cow produced very little milk, and because it could spread diseases if not collected under clean conditions.

The Yam Festival

This picture is so colourful and packed with incident that it looks like the last reel of an old film. There are the flags of many nations, soldiers, tents, elephant-tusks, warriors, ostrich feathers, spears, dancers, tom-toms and spectators.

There seems little doubt that it is West Africa, and very probably Ghana. The Ashanti kingdom there was the most advanced civilisation in Black Africa, weaving beautiful cloth, carving ivory, and organizing festivals and entertainments.

As for the period, it is almost certainly the first quarter of the nineteenth century. This was before any illustrated magazines had appeared, and so this illustration must be a 'fold-out' page from a book.

All these people and their British Army guests are gathered to celebrate the existence of the yam. West Africa is the birthplace of this food, where it is so important to the diet that it is honoured in religious and other ritual festivals.

Potatoes and yams reached Europe at roughly the same time, but from quite different directions. While potatoes were arriving from the New World, yams were arriving from the oldest continent, Africa. And while both vegetables are eaten in most countries today, the potato is to North Americans and Europeans what the yam is to people

living in the tropical and subtropical belts all round the world.

The yam is, in fact, the most important root vegetable in the world, and is eaten even more than the potato.

It is very difficult to follow the history of the yam because there are many species, it is known by many names, the word is used for many other species, and its African birthplace denies it the pedigree of a written record. This is a pity because, while the African continent has given much to the world (including, probably, the birth of the human race) it has not given much in the way of food. It would be nice to have proof that the yam began here, but all we can say is that it is one of the only two places where it grows wild, and in the ancient language of the other (India) there is no word for it. In West Africa the word is 'nyami', and when slaves from West Africa crossed the sea to the New World they took both the yam and its name with them. There it was re-named by the Spanish 'iname', by the Portuguese 'inhame', the French 'igname', and the British 'yam'.

Whether it reached Europe directly from West Africa or in a roundabout way via America, or from both sources is not known. What we do know is that it soon spread through the tropics and was eventually carried overseas as far as Australia.

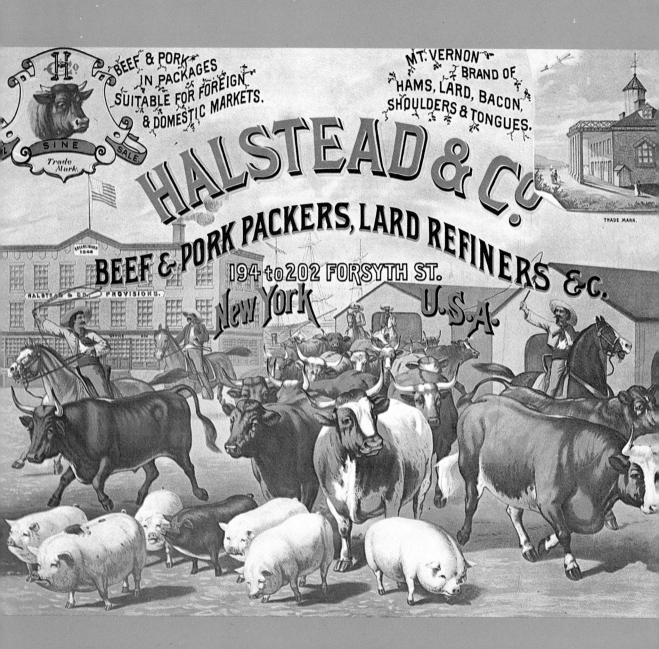

BEEF & PORK IN PACKAGES SUITABLE FOR FOREIGN & DOMESTIC MARKETS.

MT. VERNON BRAND OF HAMS, LARD, BACON, SHOULDERS & TONGUES.

TRADE MARK.

HALSTEAD & Cº

BEEF & PORK PACKERS, LARD REFINERS &c.

194 to 202 FORSYTH ST.
New York   U.S.A.

Canning Meat

This advertisement for canned meat in the 1880s shows those heroes of American folklore, the cowboys, driving cattle and pigs into a canning factory. The pigs were in the picture because Halsteads sold pork as well as beef, but it looks suspiciously as though the artist did not have his heart in them, for the cows are drawn so much better than those porky balloons whose legs can hardly bear their weight.

Bully Beef

Meat had been canned since near the beginning of the nineteenth century, and it is amazing to think that Napoleon's soldiers could have eaten bully beef. France was the first country to pack cooked meat into sealed glass bottles. By 1812 (the year of Napoleon's retreat from Moscow) a factory had been set up in England to take the idea a stage further with tinned iron containers. This opened the way for the massive export of canned beef from the prairies of America and Argentina, and mutton from the plains of Australia.

The reason for canning meat and other foods was not to make transportation easier, however, but for preservation. Meat normally goes bad within a week or so, but excluding air from food is one way of preventing decay. The meat was first placed in tins, sealed over except for a pinhole, and there cooked in liquid in a temperature of 270°F (132°C) for about three hours. Because water cannot reach this temperature, the liquid used was calcium chloride. This cooking destroyed all the germs while the air escaped through the pinhole, and then the hole was soldered over. Meat treated like this could keep for at least twenty years without going bad.

Canned Luxury

At first, preserved meat was only eaten by the rich. It cost more than fresh meat, but we must remember that since the great exodus from country to town during the Industrial Revolution, meat had always been for the wealthy. Canned meat was a luxury in the 1820s and 1830s, and it was hare pâté and truffled woodcock that was sold, rather than bully beef and mutton.

For the next twenty years, Australia was the leading canning and meat-exporting country, and Australian canned meat was less than half the price of fresh-killed meat in England. At last the poor people of industrial towns could afford this highly nutritious food.

America came on the scene rather late, but in the 1870s was producing machine-made (instead of hand-made) cans, and building huge assembly-line factories in Chicago and other cities.

JULIUS KAYSER & Co
WINE GROWERS
of Traben on the Moselle,
GERMANY.
LONDON
offices & cellars
25, SAVAGE GARDENS,
E.C.
Representative:
M. SEIFLOW.

The Fruit of the Vine

When Rome began its conquest of Europe two thousand years ago its lines of communication were rivers. By river, through the forests of France and Germany, the Romans sent in their troops and their stores. They built camps and small towns on the banks of rivers, and, to prevent guerilla warfare and ambush they cut down the dense trees. The Romans brought their civilization with them: building-skills, road-making, plumbing, canals and aqueducts, and a precious art which has stayed with us ever since – the knowledge of making wine. All the great civilizations took the vine with them: the Phoenicians to Spain, the Greeks to Italy and Rome, and the Romans to France, Germany, and Britain. Since prehistoric times, man has been eating grapes, which first appeared in Persia.

Moselle Wine

One of the rivers where the Romans settled was the Moselle, and there it is in the picture. Its banks, long cleared of trees, are ideal vineyards. The river is the best and, long ago, the only way to transport bulky wine barrels.

The scene is little changed since Roman times. The small town of Traben nestles at the foot of steep hillsides, there are quays in the river where the boats were loaded with wine to take to market. The flaxen-haired, blue-eyed, plump Rhinemaiden embodies the virtues of wine: good cheer, prosperity, and peaceful civilization.

A Popular Drink

When wine reached England, the English had an insatiable thirst for it, and as much wine was drunk then as it is now, even though there were fewer people in England then than there are in London today. Grapes were grown on a large scale in England, but the bulk of wine was imported from Bordeaux, which belonged to England at the time. The wine trade was so important that the amount a ship could carry was measured by the number of tuns (casks which held about 250 gallons) it held. A vessel which could carry sixty tuns was a 'sixty-tun ship'. That is where we get the word 'ton' today.

European settlers took the vine to South America in the sixteenth century, to South Africa in the seventeenth, and to South Australia in the nineteenth. It couldn't be grown in the United States because of a nasty little beetle called phylloxera which ate the roots. However, the goldrush of the 1860s opened up the western states, including California, where the phylloxera did not live. California is now one of the great wine-producing areas of the world.

'Maple Sugaring'

When we think of sugar, we imagine a picture of dark-skinned workers toiling in American canefields under a hot sun. However, in part of North America, and in Canada, at a certain time of year, sugar is produced from trees. The trees are maple trees, and the sugar is contained in their sap, which flows in the spring when the days are cool and the nights freezing. For the Indians of north-eastern America and nearby Canada it was the only sweetener there was, and when Europeans began to settle in America they quickly took maple sugar to their hearts. All they had to do was score the tree's bark, then hang buckets beneath for the sap to drip into. A tree might give twelve gallons of sap in a season, which would boil down to 1¼ pints of maple syrup or 3 lbs (1 kilo) of sugar. There were plenty of trees. It was always a happy, celebratory time and the people in this picture have made the work seem more like an outdoor party.

Sugar Cane

Of course, the majority of sugar comes from cane. Sugar cane came originally from India, and rich Europeans were eating cane sugar from Arab countries during the Middle Ages. The seaport city of Venice enjoyed a monopoly of the European sugar trade from the Middle East until the Portuguese navigator,

Vasco da Gama, sailed round South Africa to reach India. From then on, Portugal imported raw sugar and supplied the rest of Europe. At about the same time Columbus reached the New World, taking sugar cane with him.

From the Spanish territories of Cuba, Hispaniola, and other islands, sugar spread into the Portuguese colonies in Brazil, and then back again to other Caribbean islands, such as Dutch Surinam, British Barbados, and French Martinique and Guadeloupe. The sugar trade became so important to the island's owners that, during the wars fought for the possession of the New World, the British were able to swap the island of Surinam for New York, and to trade Guadeloupe for the whole of Canada. Sugar was the first and main cause of slaves being brought from Africa to work in the West Indies.

Sugar Beet

It was a German chemist who discovered that sugar could be extracted from beets, but no one took any notice of this discovery until Napoleon, half a century later. When the English fleet blockaded France and cut off its source of sugar from the Caribbean, he encouraged the cultivation of sugar beets. Nowadays about a third of all sugar comes from beet.

50

Tomatoes for Market

Some centuries before Cortez and his conquistadores began to plunder Central America, a Mexican peasant was working in his maize fields, and noticed a fibrous green weed trailing about the stalks of corn. He grubbed out as many as he could, but the following year they were back again, carried by natural propagation from Peru over many centuries, and by the middle of the summer they had borne small green fruits which, as the season wore on, turned quickly red. At last curiosity overtook him and he bit a piece of the fruit. His mouth filled with tangy water, and thereafter he was delighted to be able to pick the fruits and cook them in with his maize, peppers, and beans.

Golden Apples

The idea caught on, and the American farmer in the picture is taking a basket of these same fruits from his wife, to carry them away to market. They are no longer called golden apples, however – the common name for them is tomato. It took a long time for them to turn from a weed into a valuable economic crop; from an imagined poison to an important source of vitamins A and C.

This charming picture breathes the very atmosphere of the clean-living, hard-working, God-fearing, American backwood way of life. It was produced by the famous printmakers Currier & Ives who provided the printshops and the new weekly journals of America with homespun, patriotic images of the life all Americans liked to identify with.

The tomato took several thousand years to travel from its birthplace to Mexico. It needed the arrival of Europeans to take it out of the continent. In Europe it was regarded with suspicion; and considered unhealthy, or poisonous. For a long time the plant was only valued as a garden ornament, and when the fruits were reluctantly brought to the table they were recommended to be boiled for several hours!

Never Eaten Raw

However, they slowly became accepted by Europe, and eventually travelled back across the Atlantic to the continent where they had come from. Tomatoes were used cautiously in pickles and flavourings, but not until around the mid-nineteenth century did the novel idea of eating them raw come about.

When we think how often tomatoes are eaten now, it is amazing to realize they are such a recent addition to our diet. In France, a country which takes such pride in its cuisine, they did not become popular until well into the present century. Today, tomatoes are both grown and eaten in most countries of the world.

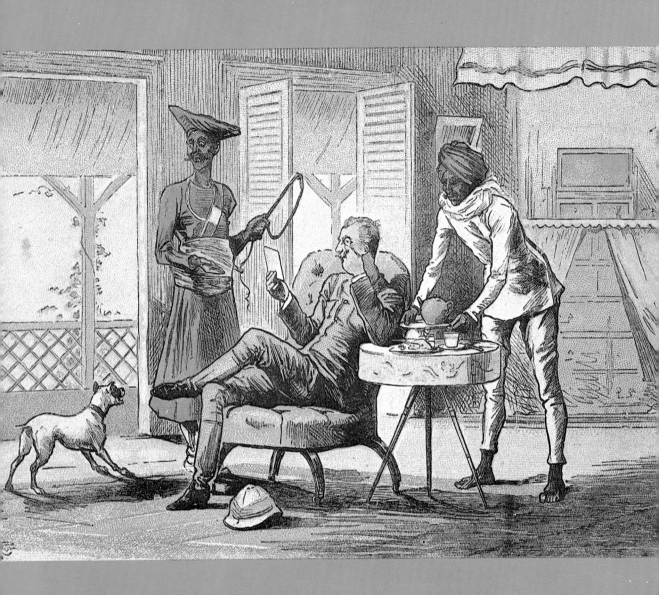

Time For Tea

In this picture, affection and disapproval are mixed in roughly equal measures. Many trappings of imperial arrogance are to be seen. The Englishman sitting while his visitor stands, his affected use of the monocle, ignoring his 'bearer' who has just brought him some refreshment (though he would certainly have noticed if he hadn't), and his contempt for the fact that the dog is barking loudly. Yet it is impossible to believe that the artist does not rather like this stuffy colonial administrator, and would not have minded drawing up a second chair and sharing his pot of tea.

Tea in China

For, of course, tea is what it has to be. Nothing could ever be allowed to stand in the way of an Englishman's tea. It is, however, odd that it was the British who introduced the cultivation of tea into India, because the Indian province of Assam is the home of the only wild tea plant to be found anywhere in the world. It was apparently ignored, however, and for at least a thousand years China was the only country that cultivated tea. By A.D. 800 the tea plant had been introduced into Japan.

Tea did not become known to Europeans until about the end of the sixteenth century, and it was another sixty or seventy years before the first tea house was opened in Exchange Alley in London. The English East India Company imported 4,713 lbs (about 2,140 kilos) of it from China in 1678, at a price only the rich could afford. One hundred years later, imports had risen to over 5½ million lbs (2,495,000 kilos).

Boston Tea Party

In 1773 the British East India Company found itself with about 17,000,000 lbs (7,700,000 kilos) of tea on its hands. So the British Government lowered the tax on tea exported to its American colonies to make it cheaper than smuggled tea. But fiery American patriots objected to such interference in their affairs, and one night they boarded the tea ships in Boston Harbour and dumped all the tea overboard. It must be the only example in history of rebellion at lower taxes. The Boston Tea Party, as it became known, was a major event leading up to the American War of Independence.

In the 1830s the East India Company lost its monopoly of the Chinese tea-trade to American shippers, whose fast sailing ships (tea-clippers) delivered the goods more quickly. At the same time tea was discovered growing wild in Assam. Chinese plants were brought to Assam and the Assam species was developed at the same time. Soon India was outstripping China in production.

Their greene corne.

Corne newly sprong.

Their sitting at meate

The face of Solomon Prayer

The horose wherin the Tombe of their Herounds standeth.

SECOTON

A Valuable Crop

This picture of a village in Central America was drawn in the early part of the sixteenth century by an English artist. He is obviously interested in the unusual plant taking up about a quarter of the picture. He had never seen this cereal before (nor had anyone else in Europe, Africa, Asia or Australia), and he would be surprised to know that it is now the second most common cereal in the world. Only rice produces more grain than maize.

You can see the maize in its three stages of growth, the young shoots, the half-grown green corn, and the mature crop with its hard husks wrapped tightly around the ears of corn. In the middle of the picture three people are tucking into a meal of it.

A Staple Diet

Maize is by far the most important food to come out of the New World. It had been responsible for turning the people of Central America from wanderers into settled societies; without it, the Inca, Aztec, and Mayan cultures would never have come into existence.

The Spanish conquerors of Central America brought it back to Europe where it was never greatly liked. 'More suitable for swine than for men', according to one writer, and indeed it is eaten today more by animls than humans all over the world – but by animals which men then eat. The Portuguese introduced it into their African colonies, where it was liked very much because Africa was poor in cereals and maize cultivates very easily and quickly. Today maize is the staple diet in Africa, but unfortunately it is comparatively poor in vitamins. In the Americas it was eaten with other, nutritious food such as tomatoes, peppers, and fish.

Poor Soil

By 1530 maize had reached the Philippines and twenty years later it was established in China. The American Government sent huge quantities of maize to feed the starving people in Russia in the early 1920s where it quickly became popular, and Russia is now the world's second largest producer (though still a long way behind America). Maize grows in poor soil with minimum cultivation, at almost any altitude wherever it can get hot sunshine and 15 inches (37.5 cm) of rain a year. It is easy to see how it has spread all over the poor countries of Asia, Africa, and South America.

The New World has given many important foods to the Old, and we would be poorer without any of them. Without maize, however, a very large portion of the world's population would not even exist.

Apples, Pears and Plums

Here is a rich man's orchard (perhaps he even lives in that castle on the hill), where he is watching the autumn picking of his fruit. He is too grand to supervise it himself. For that job he employs a steward. He gives the steward his orders and the steward passes them on to the pickers, though in fact they seem to know exactly what to do and are quietly getting on with the job.

The Fruit Orchard

It is a little difficult to see exactly what the fruit is, but a good guess would be that the trees bear apples, pears and plums. The tallest tree, on the extreme left of the picture, certainly looks like a pear tree. There are smaller trees just behind it whose red fruit could be apples, and in the four baskets there are apple-shaped fruits similar in colour to the green apples produced in France today. The tree in the middle could be plum and so, too, could the tree on the right where one of the pickers is using a stick to reach the farthest branches.

Elsewhere in the picture you can see seedlings being raised within the protection of fences, and indeed every spare plot of ground seems to be given over to fruit cultivation. Up there on the hill are more fruit trees, and that large covered wagon might be collecting the full baskets to take the fruit to be stored or bottled.

The Famous Apple

The difficulty in tracing the true history of these fruits is that their names are so loosely used. 'Apple', especially, is the name given to almost any similar fruit on first being discovered: ancient explorers or writers, on seeing a vegetable or fruit somewhere in size between a melon and a walnut, called it an apple until it was named otherwise. However, we know that apples, pears and plums probably all originated in Europe and the adjacent part of Asia and were first cultivated there between two and four thousand years ago.

The apple has a special place in folklore. In particular, we think of Eve tempted by the serpent with an apple, and it was the apple falling on Isaac Newton's head which set him wondering about the law of gravity.

There are dozens of varieties of plums in most countries of the world, and many more are produced by crossbreeding. In the ancient world there were only four.

Pears were being cultivated four thousand years ago in the temperate areas of Europe and northern Asia. They reached ancient Greece, and, soon after, Egypt and Rome. French Jesuit missionaries were the first to introduce them to America.

Acknowledgements and Sources of Pictures

cover   An illustration for the story of Abu Hasan from the book *Arabian Nights* published by Hodder & Stoughton. The artist, Edmund Dulac (1882–1953) was famous for his beautiful illustrations of traditional fairy tales. (Mary Evans Picture Library)

page 10   Cheyenne Indians hunting buffalo, from the painting by American artist Charles M. Russell. (Peter Newark's Western Americana)

page 12   This is the picture which appears on the cover.

page 14   A photograph taken in England in the 1920s. (John Topham Picture Library)

page 16   A modern colour photograph of flooded rice fields on the southern bank of the Yangtze River in China. (Xinhua News Agency)

page 18   A sixteenth-century woodcut from the work *Agricola* published in 1556. (The Mansell Collection)

page 20   A nineteenth-century advertisement for Rowntrees 'Elect' Cocoa. (Wayland Picture Library).

page 22   'Das Eiermädchen' (The Egg-girl), a nineteenth-century coloured engraving by G. Schalcken, probably from a book published in Germany. (Mary Evans Picture Library)

page 24   'Picking Peas', a coloured engraving from an 1873 issue of the journal, the *Illustrated London Almanack*. (Mary Evans Picture Library)

page 26   An illustration from an eighteenth-century book on the study of new methods of farming, published in France. (BBC Hulton Picture Library)

page 28   A coloured engraving, from a book or journal, published in about 1847. (Mary Evans Picture Library)

page 30   The cover illustration to *Cassell's Illustrated Almanack, 1870*, a nineteenth-century journal published in Britain and the United States. (The Mansell Collection)

page 32   A copy, probably made in the nineteenth century, of a seventeenth-century engraving. From a book entitled *History of the British Plantations in*

Information Sources of Further

FINDING OUT MORE

There are no museums of food as such. The best you can do is visit museums of agriculture or natural history, or ethnography (the study of different races), such as The Museum of Mankind in London. You can also look for paintings in museums and art galleries that show people eating and drinking.

When you go abroad, eat the local food and quiz the waiter and shopkeeper about where the food comes from. You can also ask the greengrocer at home about the sources of fruits and vegetables in different seasons.

The big food-processing and importing companies have public relations departments which are helpful about where food is grown. Some of the more important ones are:

Elders & Fyffes, London. (Fruit).
Kellog Company of Great Britain, Manchester. (Cereals).
Rowntree Mackintosh, York. (Chocolate).
Brooke Bond Oxo, London. (Coffee and tea).
Findus, Croydon. (Fish)
McDougalls, Nottingham. (Wheat).

There are also trade associations and official information services:

Butter Information Council, Tonbridge, Kent.
National Dairy Council, London.
Deciduous Fruit Board, London.
Potato Marketing Board, London.
Rice Council, London.
British Sugar Bureau, London.

The Commonwealth Institute in London will tell you about the cultivation of major foods in the Commonwealth countries, such as maize, coffee, tea, cocoa, fruit, rice, sugar and wheat.

BOOKS

Encyclopedia Britannica. Most articles of food have an entry in this encyclopedia, which is in every library.

Hartley, Doreen *Food in England.* This is very good on cooking equipment and local customs as well as foods.

Johnston, A. *A Hundred Years Eating.* An interesting, short book about the foods eaten in the eighteenth and nineteenth centuries.

Root, Waverley *Food.* This is an encyclopedia containing hundreds of readable and entertaining essays about food in history and literature.

Tannahill, Reay *History of Food* (????). This is a more academic book than Waverley Root's, but full of good historical ideas and interesting pictures.

Whitlock, Ralph *Farming in History* (Wayland, Picture History series). This gives twenty-four examples of ways of farming from Saxon times to the twentieth century.

Novels often have more about food in them than history books do, especially the nineteenth-century ones. You can't read Charles Dickens for long before the characters are sitting down to an entertaining dish or meal. Shakespeare, too, is rich in references to food, and tells you a lot about the customs and manners of eating in Tudor times. There are also many books on individual foods, such as cheese, bread, wine or herbs.

Glossary

Aztecs: The race which founded the ancient Mexican empire.

Carbon 14 date-testing: A method of dating prehistoric or ancient objects. All living, or once-living, things contain carbon 14, which is radioactive, and by measuring the amount of radiation still remaining it is possible to work out the age of the object.

Cheyenne Indian: One of the tribes native to North America.

Corn: The name for any cereal plant such as wheat or maize, or the grain from those plants.

Crop: The produce of cultivated land (see below).

Crossbreeding: Using the male and female from two different species to produce offspring which should inherit the best characteristics of their parents.

Cultivated land: Land which is prepared and tended specially for growing crops.

Domesticated animal: An animal, once wild, that has been tamed by man for his use.

Famine: This is the widespread, desperate shortage of food.

Far East: The countries of eastern Asia, in particular China and Japan.

Mammal: An animal that suckles its young.

Medieval: The adjective which describes the period of the Middle Ages (see below).

Middle Ages: The name for the period from the eleventh to fifteenth centuries.

Middle East: Loosely, the mainly Moslem countries lying between the Mediterranean's east coast and Iran.

Monopoly: To have the sole rights and exclusive control over something, such as trade.

Monsoon: The monsoon season is one of heavy rainfall, often flooding, in countries in the region of the Indian Ocean.

Moors: The race of mixed Arab, Spanish and Berber origin, who founded the Arab-Andalusian civilization.

New World: The name given to the continent of North and South America, discovered in the fifteenth century.

Nutritious: A food that is nutritious contains a great deal of goodness and nourishment.

Old World: The continents of Europe, Asia, and Africa, which were known before the discovery of the New World.

Prehistoric: The period of time before written records began.

Propagation: The multiplication of a species of plant or animal over a wide area.

Reap: To harvest, or gather in, a crop.

Scythe: A sharp cutting tool once used in the harvest, but now replaced by machinery.

Staple diet: A diet consisting of one main item of food, such as rice or maize.

Stone Age: The stage of development in man's history, when stone tools and weapons were used.

Temperate: A region is described as temperate when it has a mild climate, between tropical and polar.

Index